STO

ACPL ITEM
DISCARDED

ALLEN COUNTY PUBLIC LIBRARY
3 1833 00764 7818

ELY S. PARKER
Spokesman for the Senecas

Other books by Harold W. Felton

Legends of Paul Bunyan
Pecos Bill: Texas Cowpuncher
John Henry and His Hammer
Fire-Fightin' Mose
Bowleg Bill: Seagoing Cowpuncher
Cowboy Jamboree: Western Songs and Lore
New Tall Tales of Pecos Bill
Mike Fink: Best of the Keelboatmen
A Horse Named Justin Morgan
Sergeant O'Keefe and His Mule, Balaam
William Phips and the Treasure Ship
Pecos Bill and the Mustang
Jim Beckwourth, Negro Mountain Man
Edward Rose, Negro Trail Blazer
True Tall Tales of Stormalong
Nat Love, Negro Cowboy
Big Mose: Hero Fireman
Mumbet: The Story of Elizabeth Freeman
James Weldon Johnson
Gib Morgan, Oil Driller

ELY S. PARKER
Spokesman for the Senecas

HAROLD W. FELTON

Illustrated by Lorence F. Bjorklund

DODD, MEAD & COMPANY
New York

Copyright © 1973 by University of Nebraska Foundation

All rights reserved

No part of this book may be reproduced in any form
without permission in writing from the publisher

ISBN: 0–396–06736–0

Library of Congress Catalog Card Number: 72–7748

Printed in the United States of America

CO. SCHOOLS
C805783

To Grace and John

CONTENTS

INTRODUCTION

A CENTURY ago the need for an introduction to Ely S. Parker probably would not have been necessary, for he was well known. In 1873, he was forty-five and had been a leader in the unequal struggle for Indian freedom and dignity since he was fourteen years old. He would continue the battle until his death in 1895.

A member of an oppressed race, he had, by hard work and determination, obtained a good education. He had assisted Lewis H. Morgan—who was to become renowned as a pioneer investigator of the history of American Indians—in preparing a book, *The League of the Ho-de-no-sau-nee or Iroquois*, which is generally accepted to be not merely the first, but the leading work of its kind. Carl Resek, in *Lewis Henry Morgan, American Scholar* (1960), writes, "Today Morgan's book remains the most comprehensive single volume on New York Indians," and "Morgan created the science of anthropology." Francis Parkman, explorer, historian, and author of *The Oregon Trail*, in reviewing the book, declared, "It is a production of singular merit." The book was called "remarkable" by Francis Wayland, the prominent educator and the President of Brown University. John Wesley Powell, early ethnologist, director of the United States Geological Survey, and explorer of the Colorado River, declared it to be "The first scientific account of an Indian tribe given to the world."

Ely Samuel Parker had been a Brigadier General in the Union Army in the Civil War. In 1869, he was appointed the first Indian Commissioner of Indian Affairs. He occupied an important place in the development of President Ulysses S. Grant's Peace Policy, then and now widely admired.

Charles H. Coe in *Red Patriots* (1898) says that policy was "one of the brightest chapters in General Grant's administration as President of the United States."

The Peace Policy recognized the past improper treatment of Indians, contemplated their security on reservations large enough for their needs, and looked toward territorial governments for their protection. The policy included Indian education in agriculture and other sciences and arts to enable them to join the onrushing tide of the new civilization that would otherwise overwhelm them. Jennings C. Wise in *The Red Man in the New World Drama* (edited and revised by Vine Deloria, Jr., 1971) describes the "Grant-Parker plan" as one to "emancipate the Indians from economic slavery of the aboriginal communal system." He adds, "Grant's Indian policy alone would mark him for posterity as a great man."

The reach and purpose of Grant's Indian peace policy is contained in an affirmative answer to a query he presented in his Second Inaugural Address: "The moral view of the question should be considered and the question asked, cannot the Indian be made a useful and productive member of society by proper teaching and treatment?"

It has been said that Grant's peace policy failed, but it might more accurately be said that it was killed by the influences that had long preyed on America's first inhabitants.

Parker's service and ability were recognized by his own people. He was a Tonawanda Seneca and hence a member of one of the Six Nations that made up the Iroquois. At the age of twenty-three he was given the title of Chief Sachem of the Iroquois, and the name Do-ne-ho-ga-wa, Keeper of the Western Door. It was their highest office.

These few words should serve to establish the credentials of one of our most outstanding native Americans, and one who did not gain his fame on the warpath. He was one who made the incredibly long and difficult journey from one civilization to another, and who met and competed with white men on their own ground, using their rules.

Ely Parker lived a life that glows with ability and grit.

Chapter 1

THE READER

"WHAT'S YOUR name, boy?"

"Eh? What say?"

"Your name? Your name?"

"Name?"

"Listen, will you? Joe, we certainly have a dumb one here."

"Perhaps he doesn't speak English, Sam." The English officer turned to the small Indian boy standing before him. "You speak English?" he demanded.

"English? I speak," the boy answered, his dark eyes sparkling.

"All right. Your name. N-a-m-e." He spelled the shouted letters out slowly.

"Ah. Name. Name Ha-sa-no-an-da." The boy smiled.

"What does that mean in English? Mean? Understand?"

"Mean in English. Mean like with book, look at book.

Name mean read." The English words, long away from his tongue, came slowly.

"He can't talk, Joe. He's dumb."

"No, perhaps he can. What does it mean?"

"Indian name mean in English, one who reads. The Reader," the boy said earnestly. He pointed to the officers. "You Sam. You Joe. What those names mean?"

"We are officers. Call us Lieutenant," was the brusk reply.

The boy was alone, in Canada, working for the English army as a stable hand and horse herder. But he had been on his own for two years. Tall men, even officers in fancy uniforms, did not frighten him. "Yes. Sure. But what those names mean?" he asked pleasantly.

There was a pause. "Blessed if I know," said Sam.

"It isn't the same thing at all," said Joe.

"Why not? My name means, The Reader. What your names mean?"

"Your name may mean that you are a reader, but I doubt it."

"That's good. The Reader! I'll wager he has never even seen a book."

"We'll call him Stupid, for short."

"I say there, Stupid, I always thought you redskins were named for something you did awfully well."

"He can't speak well. There's little chance he can read well, if at all."

Ha-sa-no-an-da caught the drift of what they were saying, though he did not understand all the words. He had read books. Some time ago, it was true, but there are other things to read. The signs in the woods that are known to the trapper and hunter, the signs that tell the weather. Oh, if he only had the words to tell them.

"He is a mule driver. Not good for anything else. Indians can't learn. Everyone knows that."

"I have English name."

"So you have an English name, have you? Stole it probably."

"Yes. English name is Parker."

"Parker? Where did you get that?"

The boy looked puzzled. "My father," he said at length.

"No, Parker isn't your name. Your name is Stupid."

Ha-sa-no-an-da listened to the sounds they made. Most of them fell on his ear without meaning, like the noise of falling trees, the rush and roar of a waterfall, the crack of whips, the thumps of horses' hooves on hard ground. But he understood enough to feel he was not admired by these tall, well-dressed English officers. He keenly felt the scorn for him in their voices.

A serious look came over his face. He was a Seneca, a Tonawanda Seneca, and the Senecas were one of the Six Nations of the Iroquois. His mother was of the Wolf Clan, one of the great clans of the tribe. He was a descendant of the

Seneca prophet, Handsome Lake, and of Cornplanter, the heroic Iroquois leader, and he was a grandson of the famous chief, Red Jacket. These English officers should know that Red Jacket fought with the English in the war with the Colonies; that he made a treaty with General Washington and received a silver medal; that he was a great orator, the greatest Iroquois orator.

He could never make them understand that in the Revolutionary War his ancestors captured a man named Parker and that the captive in gratitude gave his name to the Indians who saved his life and treated him well. And he really could read books. At least he read them before he stopped going to school, and he—

"Got a first name?"

"First name?"

"Yes. A first name."

"Ha-sa-no-an-da. But I have other name," he said suddenly. "Other name is Ely."

"Ely?"

"Yes. But I like Ha-sa-no-an-da more."

"You do, eh? Well, I like Stupid more."

A torrent of Indian words poured from the boy. The two officers broke into laughter at the strange sounds and the deep seriousness of the dark face. They didn't know he was saying in his native language all of the things he could not say in English.

When they recovered from their fit of laughing, Sam said, "Joe, I honestly never heard or saw anything so funny before."

"Nor I. Stupid, there, is filled with a lot of something, even though it isn't English."

"All right, Stupid. Let's go. We have a long journey. These horses and mules have to be driven to Hamilton." Ha-sa-no-an-da stood solemnly, his face covered by a dark cloud of thoughtfulness.

The officers mounted their horses. Ha-sa-no-an-da understood the action if not the words. He sprang to his horse's back. "Ho! Hi ho!" he cried. The horses and mules in the grazing herd lifted their heads and began to move.

Another long journey between London and Hamilton began, but the beautiful Canadian countryside seemed strangely dull to the young Indian, though the sun was shining brightly.

Chapter 2

HA-SA-NO-AN-DA MAKES UP HIS MIND

HA-SA-NO-AN-DA was troubled, and as the days passed, his heart became sad.

He was the butt of jokes and scorn. These English officers could not seem to understand his name. It was not Stupid. It was Ha-sa-no-an-da.

He had earned his name in the mission school at Tonawanda in New York State. He was the best reader in his class. He liked school. His parents wanted him to go. But he didn't understand what good it would do. He didn't want to be a farmer or operate a sawmill as his father did.

He certainly didn't want to live like a white man. He didn't like what he saw of them or what he heard of them. In 1838, they had come to the Indians with demands for a treaty. They came with bribes, with alcohol. They were destroying Indian life. They brought bickering and strife with their lust for land and property.

Although he was only ten years old, Ha-sa-no-an-da could see what happened to the Indians who had been made drunk. He had heard the stories of bribes and cheating. His own family struggled against the treaty makers. Most of the Tonawanda Senecas did.

Ha-sa-no-an-da had gone to school for a few years. The lessons were taught in English, but away from the classroom, the children spoke their native tongue.

He knew of the old Indian ways. He had seen some of the open life, of hunting, fishing, trapping, with horses, with freedom.

His own family had moved away from the old life. They lived in a house of sawed boards instead of the ruder, old-fashioned Seneca cabin of poles and elm or ash bark. He had never lived in one of the long houses that were sometimes used by several families.

His father worked as a white man worked, in a small sawmill he owned. He also farmed and raised horses. Of course the Senecas had always been farmers. That was a part of the old Indian life.

With his parents' reluctant blessing he had quit school and had gone to Canada on the Grand River, to live with friends and relatives of his mother's Wolf Clan. He made the trip north with an old companion of his father.

But soon that life began to seem empty. He worked his

way south, to the area north of Lake Erie. He got a job, working for the British army, driving horses and mules between London and Hamilton in Canada, driving mule teams, cleaning stables, freighting, doing a man's work.

He was now twelve. And he didn't know enough English to answer these officers. He couldn't defend himself, or explain himself and his people. They made fun of him and there was nothing he could do about it. He had many thoughts, but no way to make these people understand.

The burden Ha-sa-no-an-da carried became heavier. His thoughts burned inside him, struggling for freedom.

His name meant more than The Reader. It was hard to translate. Some Senecas said it meant "The Name that Leads." To others it meant "Coming to the Front." As he thought of it he came to realize that words mean a lot. He began to understand why Ha-sa-no-an-da had such a wide meaning. One must be a reader to lead. A leader is a reader. A reader is a leader. Both come to the front. He began to realize that he should go back to school and learn what other words meant and how to use them.

Slowly his new understanding became a wish. A wish became a desire. Unhappiness took the place of contentment with horses and mules, fresh air, and open country.

Then anger came, anger with the English officers who laughed at him because he couldn't speak their language as well as they did.

His anger turned inward. He determined to change the

direction of his life. It was a white man's world. He was a part of it whether he liked it or not. He couldn't hide from it. He couldn't escape from it. He would go back to school and make up for the time he had lost. He would learn to read and write and figure and speak. Never again would a white man make fun of Ha-sa-no-an-da!

Chapter 3

A MOTHER'S DREAM

HA-SA-NO-AN-DA walked back to his old home on the Tonawanda River in New York. It was well over a hundred miles and each step made his firm determination firmer still. The Reader. He had earned his name honestly. But he could not keep it if he did not deserve it. He would study hard and earn it again.

His earlier years came back to him as he walked. He remembered his first day in school. He needed a name to go in the record book. Indian names were difficult for white people to pronounce. The teacher, a Baptist clergyman, the Reverend Ely Stone, looked down at him. In the Seneca language he asked, "Ha-sa-no-an-da Parker, would you like another first name? An English one?"

The boy nodded.

"How would you like to have my name for your first name?"

The boy nodded again, eagerly.

"All right. You shall have it. It is Ely. I'll put it here in the book. Ely Parker."

Now his heart beat faster as he approached his father's house, his old home, at Indian Falls on the Tonawanda River. There was the old house, the outbuildings, and his father's small sawmill where boards were made of the trees that had given shelter to his ancestors since the beginning of time.

And there were the pastures and the horses his father owned. His father was a good farmer. The fields were well cultivated.

Ha-sa-no-an-da stepped inside the house. There was his father, William, a Tonawanda Seneca chief. And there was his mother. She too had an English name, Elizabeth Johnson. She was of a noble family, the granddaughter of a leading Sachem of the nation.

And Ely's older brother and sister, Levi and Caroline, with his younger brothers, Nicholson, Spencer, and Isaac Newton. They were there too.

"Ah, my son," said his father. "Welcome."

"Welcome, welcome," said his mother. "You look well."

"I am not well, mother," said Ha-sa-no-an-da.

"Not well? But—" Her anxious mother's eyes passed over his strong, young body.

"It is here," said the boy, placing his hands on his head. "I

am crippled by ignorance. I have come home to cure myself."

"Cure yourself? How?" asked his mother.

"With school. I want to go back to school."

"Good. Good," said William. "We have always said to our children, 'Learn all you can.' "

"When you quit school, we were sorry," said his mother. "But you went away to learn the old Indian skills in the woods in Canada. We knew the white man's ways hurt you. We are happy to have you come back home."

That night as Elizabeth Parker sat before the fire she told her children of the birth of the boy who had just come back home, of Ha-sa-no-an-da. Before he was born she had a dream. The snow was falling. Suddenly the clouds were swept back. A rainbow appeared, and was broken in two, high in the sky. One end of the rainbow rested in English letters, like those above the shops in the white man's city of Buffalo.

She went to a man who could see inside of dreams. The old Indian used his charms and his medicine and thought about the dream. Then he told her:

"A son will be born to you who will be distinguished among his own nation as a peace-maker; he will become a white man as well as an Indian. He will be a wise white man, but will never desert his Indian people . . . his name will reach from the east to the west, the north to the south. . . . His sun will rise on Indian land and set on the white man's land. Yet the ancient land of his ancestors will fold him in death."

Chapter 4

THE IROQUOIS

IN THE DAYS that followed, at home and at school, Ely learned more of the history of the Senecas and Iroquois.

In the beginning there were five tribes living in the Mohawk River Valley. Although they spoke the same language, they made war on each other.

The Mohawks were in the east, at the Hudson River. To the west were the Oneidas, then the Onondagas, followed by the Cayugas, with the Senecas on the extreme west, at the Niagara River.

There was among them a young brave named Ha-yo-went-ha, whom the whites would latter call Hiawatha. His grandmother was the daughter of the moon. His father was the west wind.

Hiawatha could shoot arrows so far and so high and so fast that he could put ten arrows in the air before the first one he shot hit the ground. And no brave could run faster than he.

When he shot an arrow in level flight, he could run so fast he could reach the target before the arrow did.

Those stories were legends, perhaps, that arose out of the life of a great man and the ideals of a nation. It was not easy to tell where the legends ended and history began.

When Hiawatha grew older he saw that war between the five nations of the Iroquois was wrong. What could be done where the occupations of men were fishing, hunting, and war? How could peace and happiness be brought to them?

At that time the Iroquois were attacked by enemies from the north. They were fighting each other and they were fighting their new enemies. They were being overcome by those who came from the north.

In distress the people called on Hiawatha. He counseled the five Iroquois nations to make peace with each other and join together to resist their enemies. The Confederation of the Five Nations was formed.

The Iroquois called themselves "People of the Long House." They thought of themselves as living in a long house with separate rooms and fires, stretching the length of the trail that joined them, between the Hudson and the Niagara Rivers.

When the Tuscaroras joined the League of the Iroquois in 1722, their land was between the Oneidas and the Onondagas and along the south of the Five Nations.

Each of the nations was divided into clans. The major clans were Bear, Wolf, Turtle, and Beaver, followed by Deer,

Snipe, Heron, and Hawk. In addition to the chiefs, the clans were represented in the councils by Sachems, the highest officers. Some clans had more than one. There were fifty Sachems in all. Two of the most important were Senecas and the leader of these was Do-ne-ho-ga-wa, "Keeper of the Western Door."

Under the guidance of Hiawatha, the Iroquois learned the arts, agriculture, and medicine.

Among the Iroquois no one owned the land or water, the air or game. These were gifts to all from the creator. Their religion taught kindness, hospitality, friendship. All Iroquois were brothers. Strangers were welcome. Food was given to them.

No doors were locked. A broom outside the door was a sign no one was home. No one broke into a house. There was no cause to steal because there was no need. There was plenty for everyone.

For more than a century and a half, the Iroquois had stopped the white man. They had prevented him from taking all the land along the Mohawk River Valley. It had been a losing battle, but they had yielded slowly, at great cost to themselves and to the forces that attacked them.

Over the years large amounts of their land had been taken by conquest or by purchase for slight payment. The Indians were confined to reservations, but the white men wanted more and still more of their land. They were still fighting, trying to keep the small territory left to them.

The white men came with another religion and with civilization and with ideas of property. The days when all the people talked with one tongue were almost gone. The forked tongue was on the rise.

Chapter 5

BACK TO SCHOOL

ELY ENTERED the mission school for the second time. "It may not be easy for you because you are much older and much bigger than the other students," the teacher said.

"Then I must learn more and learn it more fast," Ely replied.

"It may discourage you when you see smaller children doing things you cannot do."

"If I am bigger, then I must do better," Ely said.

And he did. Books were his constant companions. He devoured knowledge. No fact was too large or too small for him.

All of the Iroquois nations, except the Oneidas and some of the Tuscaroras, became allies of the British in the Revolutionary War. These Iroquois felt they should oppose the American settlers who had gradually been moving into their land for many years. Then, too, they had fought with the British in the wars with the French.

CO. SCHOOLS
C805783

In 1779, in response to Seneca raids, the American General John Sullivan was commanded to "chastise and humble the Six Nations." This he did, ruthlessly destroying forty villages, thousands of bushels of corn in the fields and in granaries, as well as gardens, apple and pear trees, everything within the reach of his army, hunting survivors like wild beasts.

Most of the Seneca lands which lay in the beautiful, fertile country between Seneca Lake and the Niagara River were taken by the whites. But the Treaty of Canandaigua in 1794 stated that what land the Indians then possessed would remain theirs forever until they sold it. It could not be taken from them.

They were put on reservations in a dozen areas in western New York. The larger were on Buffalo Creek, the Tonawanda, the Allegheny, and the Cattaraugus Rivers.

The Senecas fought on the side of the United States in the War of 1812, saying in their declaration, "We are few in number, and can do but little, but our hearts are good."

By 1837, when Ely was nine years old, the Iroquois lands in the four largest reservations contained about 100,000 acres.

The Ogden Land Company claimed the Seneca land under old treaties, which, it claimed, gave a "pre-emptive" right to buy the land. Political pressures to take the Indian lands were immense. Fraud, deceit, bribes, and alcohol—a vicious drug that overcame good judgment on the part of the Indians—were brought into play.

Through these means, treaties and agreements to sell were signed by some irresponsible Indians in 1838. But the Tonawanda Senecas did not sign. They could not be bribed, or fed alcohol. Their names were forged. They remembered the old rules. No chief owned the land. They all owned it together. The Great Spirit had given it to them. No person could sell it or sign it away. Nor could a majority, because it was owned by all.

Some of the Indians, dismayed and discouraged, left for the western reservations where the government as well as the Land Company wanted them to go. Most of the Tonawanda Senecas did not leave. They stayed on their land. Often they were forced to fight off government officials and agents of the Land Company.

This was the life of the Indians that Ha-sa-no-an-da had left when he was ten years old, and returned to two years later. But now he had a purpose. His goal was to become able to meet the white man on his own ground and, using the white man's rules and language, prove he was equal or, perhaps, a better man.

Chapter 6

THE YOUNG INTERPRETER

THE PEOPLE of the Seneca nation watched with pride as Ely went to Yates Academy after he had learned all the mission school had to offer.

As a student at Yates, he spoke in public for temperance, against the drug that was alcohol, that had done so much to debase Indian culture and which had robbed his people. The young orator brought to white people the story of his ancestors.

Ely's brother Nicholson and his sister Carrie went to school at Pembroke in Genesee County. The two brothers exchanged their essays and speeches by mail. Thus each benefited from the work done by the other.

The teen-age boy was able to bring his talents to use as an interpreter and as a leader. He was called upon by his nation to go to Albany and to Washington with Indian delegations to help in their fight against treaties obtained from them by fraud and deceit.

A well-phrased appeal to President John Tyler was made in June of 1842, bearing his name as interpreter. A dozen chiefs signed with their marks. Ely Samuel Parker was only fourteen years old.

On these missions, with his new command of the English language, he presented the Indians' arguments to politicial leaders. In Washington, over a period of years, he spoke to Henry Clay, John Calhoun, Daniel Webster, President Tyler, President James Polk, and other government officials. The young Seneca was entertained in the White House one New Year's Day by Mrs. Polk. Another day he went for a ride with her in her carriage.

He was well received and was listened to gravely as he stood before those in power and explained the need for justice for Indians. But the lust for the fertile Seneca land was great and a constantly moving whirlwind of politics withheld success.

Although success was never in clear view, Ha-sa-no-an-da and the others working for the Indian nation did not stop presenting the story of the rightness of the Seneca cause and the wrongs that had been done to them.

The Tonawanda Senecas were greatly impressed by Ely's progress in school. They were pleased with his clear mind and his forcefulness when he spoke for them. They helped his family in paying for his education. They never before had a spokesman educated in the ways of the white man and the Indian alike.

Many thought him a genius, forgetting that genius and hard work go hand in hand. They hoped for him to become a lawyer who would be able to represent them in the strange ways of the white man's laws.

Chapter 7

LEWIS MORGAN, FRIEND

ONE DAY IN 1844, while in Albany with a group of Seneca chiefs, arguing for their nation's rights, Ely went into a bookstore.

As he browsed through the books, selecting several he thought he could afford, he brushed against a young man as they both reached for the same volume.

"I am so sorry. My apologies," said Ely.

The young man said the same words at the same time. They laughed.

"What is your particular interest?" the young man asked.

"Everything," Ely replied.

"That is an enormous field."

"Yes, I know, but I have a lot to do. I started late," Ely said.

"I started early, but I have a great deal to do too."

"My greatest interest is the Seneca nation," Ely said thoughtfully. "But first, I must have an education."

"Naturally. Everyone needs an education. You are an Indian?"

"Yes. A Seneca."

"What brings you to Albany? I hope that is not too personal a question."

"Not at all. I am here with some of the chiefs, trying to get help from the State of New York. Many people want to send us west you know."

"Yes. I know. I am much interested in the Iroquois, in all of the Six Nations."

"Not in moving us to the parched plains of Kansas, I trust. The government is trying to make us go there."

"No. Not I. I am interested not only in their survival here in New York, but in their religion, their customs, arts, laws, language, beliefs, political and social organization, their total culture."

"Culture? That is interesting. Not many people realize we have a culture."

"I know. It is a sad thing too. And my interest remains even though my grandfather fought with Sullivan when he broke the power of the Iroquois. He received six hundred acres of Iroquois land for five years of service with the Continental army."

The young man was, Ely judged, ten years older than he. He was a lawyer and was about to open his office in Rochester. He had been born and reared at Aurora, New York. He had been educated at the Cayuga Academy there, and at Union College. He had read law for three years and had been admitted to the bar. His name was Lewis Morgan.

Ely told Morgan of his life and his ambitions. He took his new friend to the hotel and interpreted as Morgan talked with the Seneca chiefs in the delegation. Lewis Morgan came back every day the Indians stayed in Albany, learning all he could of the Iroquois Confederacy and the tribes it was composed of.

The Senecas had some good friends, a number of ministers, the Quakers, some businessmen, and politicians who were aware of the problems the red men faced. These friends of the Indians were moved by sympathy and a desire for justice. Lewis Morgan was a man who didn't want to convert them or make them into farmers or businessmen. He didn't consider them "savages" or "heathens" who should be "civilized" and "converted." He recognized them as people with ways of life that made a social system, people with a culture that had long served their purpose very well.

Lewis told Ely of the Cayuga Academy where he had organized a club of students and teachers who met and discussed social and cultural questions. It was called the Gordian Knot, recalling the ancient Greek King who tied a knot so tight that no one could untie it. It was said that whoever did would become the ruler of all Asia. Alexander the Great cut the knot with his sword and conquered the known world.

At one point Lewis Morgan said, "I am amazed that so little

has been written of the culture of Indians. There are very few books on the subject and no really good ones. It is a condition that should be corrected."

Ely, for his part, was astounded that anyone cared that much. A lasting friendship was formed and Ely began to look in a new direction. His mind turned toward Aurora, New York, and the Academy in that small city on the shores of Lake Cayuga.

Chapter 8

RED JACKET'S HEIR

The next year Ely Parker began his studies at Cayuga Academy. It was the autumn of 1845.

His friend Morgan introduced him to the members of the Gordian Knot. The intellectual discussions pleased Ely, as did the members' evident interest in the Iroquois.

He made a suggestion: Use the group to study and help the Indians. It was accepted with enthusiasm. The name of the club was changed to The Grand Order of the Iroquois. The members dressed in Indian costumes for their meetings, and often met in the woods around a council fire. Their purpose became that of helping the Iroquois and saving the Senecas from the hard hand of politics, greed, and the Ogden Land Company.

As the young men in the lodge left school, they organized new lodges, establishing them throughout the State of New

York and in other states. Ely Parker and Lewis Morgan had set a force in motion.

In 1844, the Quakers made a study of methods of the Ogden Land Company in forcing the Senecas to sign away their native soil. They said: "After exhaustive investigation . . . the Committee became thoroughly satisfied of the revolting fact, that in order to drive these poor Indians from their lands, deception and fraud had been practiced to an extent, perhaps, without parallel in the dark history of oppression and wrong to which the aborigines of our country had been subjected."

Ely spoke out wherever he could find an audience. The vigor and clarity of his ideas and his command of English are evident in a speech he made at seventeen years of age when he spoke at one of the first meetings of The Grand Order of the Iroquois. He said: "Our America is in the hands of God. . . . It is true that religion and learning and liberty have here their homes, but the principles of justice have governed neither the nation nor the people. . . . The voice of a once powerful people, owners of the soil upon which the monuments of America's glory are reared, are crying to the Great Spirit to revenge their wrongs. . . . It is no pleasant task to reproach you, but my own nation is now veiled in sorrow by the perfidy of the white man. . . . Do you love your lands? So does the Indian. . . ."

His five years of study since he entered the mission school for the second time had not been wasted. The Senecas clearly

had found a voice to speak for them. Ha-sa-no-an-da, The Reader, was deserving of his name, and the blood of Red Jacket, the orator, flowed in his veins.

Because his people needed him, Ely left Cayuga Academy and went to Washington to take charge of the Senecas' campaign to be relieved of the fraudulent treaties. It was March, 1846.

The eighteen-year-old boy developed the arguments and gave voice to them. They had not signed the treaties; they had, in fact, refused to sign; the Indians who had signed were bribed or drugged with alcohol; although the Ogden Land Company had "pre-emptive" rights that permitted them to buy the land, the Tonawanda Senecas had not sold it. They were largely dependent on agriculture and hunting. Their methods of farming and the lack of game would make it impossible for them to make a living in Kansas where the government proposed to send them.

Petitions were sent to Washington by the Tonawanda Senecas and the many white people who believed they had been wronged. Meetings were held wherever possible. Ely presented the petitions and discussed them with Congressional committees, the Office of Indian Affairs, the President.

Uncertain as to their future, many Senecas lost interest in their farms. What was the use of raising a crop if someone might come and take the land before it was harvested? Why repair a house or a barn?

Discouragement drove many of them to alcohol, the drug that brought so much evil to them. But the promise of help it seemed to offer was never fulfilled. It only made matters worse.

Some of the Senecas decided they could not fight the tremendous powers that faced them. They gave up. They sold their property at low prices and began the long journey to the Kansas reservation. Two-thirds of those who started on the perilous trail died on their way to their new homes.

The government refused to set aside the treaties, saying that to do so "would not only tend to unsettle the whole of our Indian policy but would open a field of interminable difficulties, embarrassment, and expense."

But Ha-sa-no-an-da and his friends did not stop. The fight went on.

Chapter 9

THE LEAGUE OF THE IROQUOIS

LEWIS MORGAN often went to Albany and to Washington with Ely, and the two young men found time for talk and study. Morgan's notebooks became full of information of Indian life, much of which Ely supplied. Morgan planned to publish a book about the Iroquois' history.

Ely and his family collected tools, art, clothing, and other objects of Indian culture which were later used as the foundation of the New York State Museum Indian Collection.

Ely began to read law in the offices of Angel and Rice in Ellicottville. But three long, hard years of study and work as a law clerk were crowned with cruel failure. The court ruled that only male, white citizens could be admitted to the bar. Ely Parker was not white, nor was he a citizen of the United States. He was an Indian. He could not become a lawyer.

The depth of his anguish seemed limitless. "What can I do?" he asked Morgan.

"Every serious person finds his place in life. You have a good educational background. It should be put to good use."

"But three years! It seems wasted."

"Learning is never wasted."

"I suppose not. They may not admit me to the bar, but they can't take my knowledge of law away from me."

Sober thought brought the answer to Ely's problem. "I will learn engineering," he declared. "I can earn a living at that. And perhaps I can find ways to help my people too."

"Engineering is not an easy subject," Lewis Morgan said.

"I know. But I have never hunted for easy subjects. Others learn engineering. So can I. It is a good profession. I will master it."

Ely took the necessary engineering courses at Rensselaer Institute. His grades were good and upon completion of the course he found a job at Rochester, helping improve the Erie Canal.

"In one sense it turns out for the best," Ely said.

"Things usually do," Lewis replied.

"We are both here in Rochester and our work on your book can go on. So can our work for the Senecas."

There came a day in 1851 when Ely called at Lewis' home. He was met at the door by his smiling friend. "It is finished at last," Lewis said, unable to conceal his excitement.

"You have the book?" Ely asked.

"Yes. Here it is." Lewis proudly handed a new volume to his friend. It bore the title, *The League of the Ho-de-no-sau-nee or Iroquois.*

Ely opened the book. His eyes, fixed on the page, grew moist.

"You don't look like a calm, emotionless redskin to me," Lewis said with a laugh.

"I can't help it," Ely replied with a smile. "I am overwhelmed by pride and happiness." He read the dedication:

TO
HA-SA-NO-AN-DA
(ELY S. PARKER)
A SENECA INDIAN
This Work,
The Materials of Which are the Fruit of
Our Joint Researches,
Is Inscribed:
In Acknowledgment of the Obligations, and
In Testimony of the Friendship of
THE AUTHOR

Ely turned the pages as he read on. His voice caught as he read the introduction:

"It remains for the author to acknowledge his obligations to

Ely S. Parker, Ha-sa-no-an-da, an educated Seneca Indian, to whom this volume is inscribed. He is indebted to him for invaluable assistance during the whole progress of the research, and for a share of the materials. His intelligence, and accurate knowledge of the institutions of his forefathers, have made his friendly services a peculiar privilege."

Ely was happy that the knowledge of the Iroquois' past would be saved for people to read about. He was proud that he had a part in keeping the memory of the Iroquois bright.

Chapter 10

GRAND SACHEM

THE IMPROVEMENT of the Erie Canal gave Ely a good position as an engineer. He lived near his parents and the Tonawanda Senecas, and he kept in close touch with them.

A day came when Ha-sa-no-an-da was called to the council fire, at a meeting of the Sachems. They were the chief councilors, the keepers of the faith, the guardians of the ancient wisdom. This day they were in their finest costumes with the tribal totems. Chiefs and women and warriors were present. It was the most solemn moment in the life of the Iroquois. They were gathered in Grand Council to celebrate the funeral rites of the last Grand Sachem, John Blacksmith, and to elect a new leader.

The council fire was kindled. The Sachems, in double file, sang the death song. Other traditional songs and dances were repeated.

New chiefs were elected and instructed in their duties.

And the new Grand Sachem was named. He was Ha-sa-no-an-da, The Reader, a young man who had gone so far in little time and who had done so much for his people.

The long, white and purple wampum belt, symbol of his office and of the unity of the Iroquois, was handed to him with all ceremony. The silver medal that had first been the gift of President George Washington to Red Jacket was given to him.

With these symbols of authority went the love and gratitude of his people. A new name was also given him–Do-ne-ho-ga-wa, the Keeper of the Western Door of the Long House. He had received the greatest honor the Iroquois could give.

It was 1852. Do-ne-ho-ga-wa was twenty-four years old.

Chapter 11

PROMOTION COMES

Ely was successful in his work. Promotion came. He was made the Chief Engineer on the Erie Canal improvement. He bought a farm near his father's land where he raised horses. He was appointed United States Indian interpreter, a position that required him to travel to the Iroquois reservations with the Indian agent.

The government's threat of removal to the western reservations still remained with the Tonawanda Senecas. Ely Parker was the active force that prevented it. The false treaties were held to be good by the government. It had been decided that the Senecas had sold their land at a ridiculously low price.

But there was something they could do to keep from being moved west. That was to buy the land back. Then they would hold it under deeds and it could not be taken from them again. It took many years of argument and negotiation, but this was finally done in 1859. The tract of land that had been set aside for them in Kansas was sold by the government, and the money received was used to buy back the Tonawanda reservation.

One of Do-ne-ho-ga-wa's major works for his people was completed with this transaction. Then, when it was over, after years of doubt, anguish, and uncertainty, the Tonawanda Senecas were secure in their homes.

But Ely still had an important job to do. It was one he did every day and did well. It was to prove that the people who had been considered "savages" were capable of moving from one civilization to another, were able to do work and take an important place in the American world of the white man. Young people could see him and know by his example that school and study could carry them away from poverty too.

Still more professional advancement came. Ely was appointed Chief Engineer on the Chesapeake and Albemarle Canal. Carrie and Nicholson had completed their education at the Albany Normal School. The other Parker children had finished their schooling too. Levi and Spencer were farmers. Isaac Newton was a teacher. His great failure was intemperance. It made him unreliable and he often sought Ely's help in getting new jobs.

Carrie married John Mountpleasant, the leading chief of the Tuscaroras. She maintained a home of culture and refinement and exercised great influence among the Iroquois.

Nicholson became the assistant of Reverend Asher Wright, a missionary. With Reverend Wright he translated the Bible into Seneca and, with him, prepared a Seneca grammar.

"My new position will take me away from New York. Can you take care of my farm?" Ely asked his brother Nicholson.

"Certainly. You saw me through my education with Carrie, didn't you? You saw us all through school," Nicholson replied.

"I hate to leave my colts. Take good care of them," Ely said.

"Indeed I will," Nicholson replied.

Ely went to Virginia on his new position. He made the surveys, designed the new Chesapeake Canal, and supervised the first months of construction. Then a better offer came. He became Construction Engineer for the United States Government Light House District of the Western Great Lakes. He moved to Illinois.

He was a quiet man, but could speak with vigor and clarity when it was necessary. He was tall, deep chested, with powerful muscles, as lean in appearance as a two-hundred-pound man can be. He was a superior horseman, having been close to horses all his life. He was excellent at Indian sports when he was a boy. As he grew older one of his great interests was billiards and he was a splendid player.

Ely had learned early in life to be careful in the use of force because of his great strength. A stranger, prompted by too much whiskey, once challenged him in a hotel lobby in Buffalo. He was not a small man and most people would have thought it would be an even fight.

"Want to fight?" the stranger said, with clenched fists ready.

"No, of course not," said Ely.

"Coward, are you?"

"Let's say yes, and let it go at that," Ely said as he began to move away.

But the stranger was not to be discouraged. "Just what I thought. Yellow-bellied redskin!" he cried as he seized Ely by the coat sleeve and turned him around and made a lunge for him.

There seemed no way to avoid contact any longer. Ely grabbed the man around the shoulders and held his arms tight. His opponent was helpless. Suddenly the stranger let out a strange yell and stopped resisting. Ely let him go and the man silently walked away.

A few days later the same man approached him again. "I want to talk to you," the man said.

"That's a better idea than wanting to fight," Ely said with a smile.

"Look at this." He took off his coat and shirt. His arms and chest were black and blue. "See what you did to me? I could not use my arms for two days. I think you should pay me," he said. "And you should pay me for my coat too. You broke the seams around the sleeves."

"I feel sorry for you, but I merely defended myself. You were the one who started it. You are lucky I didn't return your attack," Ely said.

One evening, with a group of friends, Ely went to a dance in Norfolk when he was working on the Chesapeake Canal. He was stopped at the door and denied admittance. "No blacks allowed," the man said.

Ely saw no need to explain that he was a red man and not a black man. The notion that colors of men made a difference in their character or in their social or business lives was distasteful to him. He solved the problem by picking the man up by the seat of his pants with one hand and his coat collar with the other, lifting him over the railing of the low platform on which they were standing and dropping him to the floor. His party then entered the ball room and had a pleasant evening.

When Ely first went to Illinois, an innkeeper tried to push him into the street. Ely broke the man's grasp, but he attacked again. Ely then seized the man's arms and whirled him around until the innkeeper's feet were extended out straight. After a few moments, he stopped and helped the dizzy man to a chair. The innkeeper sat silently until his head cleared. Then he looked up with a grin. "I never saw that happen before. You are a mighty strong man," he said.

"I don't really know how strong I am," Ely admitted. "I'm always at a loss when a man comes at me. I don't want to hurt him, and it isn't easy to do something that won't cause injury."

"As far as I'm concerned, I won't try again. Shake," he said as he arose and put out his hand.

Chapter 12

ELY MEETS GRANT

As DO-NE-HO-GA-WA, the Keeper of the Western Door of the Long House of the Iroquois, and as Chief Sachem, Ely Parker had a certain amount of fame. He liked good conversation and got along easily with strangers. A member of the Wolf Clan, the name of Wolf was given to him by many of his new friends.

His work as an engineer took him to Galena, Illinois. One evening while walking home to his boardinghouse he heard a muffled noise as he passed a dark street. Three men were struggling. In the dark shadows, he saw it was two against one, and the one was a small man.

"Come. Come, stop this," he cried as he seized the two larger men and held them apart in an iron grasp.

"What is the trouble here?" Ely asked.

"They attacked me."

"Why?"

"For money, I suppose. But heaven knows I don't have much of that."

The two men struggled to be free. "What have you got to say?" Ely demanded.

No answer came. The two were busy trying to escape. Ely released his hold. They dashed down the street as fast as though a whole tribe of Senecas were after them with scalping knives.

The small man put out his hand. "My name is Grant," he said. "Thank you for saving me from those footpads."

"They had you outnumbered."

The two young men walked home together. Ely discovered that his new friend's full name was Ulysses S. Grant. He was a clerk in his father's leather and hardware store in Galena. He was a West Point graduate and had served with the United States Army in the Mexican war as a captain. Like Ely, Grant had an engineering education.

They got along very well together. They both talked well, but silence did not bore them. They both liked horses and Grant played a fair game of billiards.

The young men of Galena were interested in the growing difficulties between the Northern and Southern states. On April 13, 1861, news came that Fort Sumter was fired upon the day before. The War Between the States began. Each man, in his own way, looked to his future.

"I'm going right in," said Grant. "I have been educated for

LIVERY

war at the government's expense. It is my duty to go, although I don't like war. There comes a time when it may be necessary."

"I don't like it either," Ely agreed. "But there are times when it seems nothing else will do. You are a West Point graduate. The army will want you. But what can I do?"

"Military engineers will be in great demand. You should have no trouble," said Ulysses. "And you should have a commission. Your training requires it. The government needs officers with your abilities."

"I must help my country. If my talents are needed, I will offer them. I will quit my position, go back to New York and ask the Governor for permission to raise a regiment."

Grant's offer of his services to the army was not accepted for some time, but he began training local troops at once and was appointed a Colonel. A short time later he was made a Brigadier General.

Ely resigned his engineer's post. Following a Seneca custom, he spoke to his father. "I think I ought to serve my country, just as you did in the War of 1812. I ask your permission."

"Your brother Newton has already received my permission. He has enlisted in the Union Army as a private. Will you receive a commission?"

"I should. I am an engineer, and engineer officers are badly needed."

"Isaac Newton's education was in literature. There is no demand for literary skills in the officer ranks. That is why he is a private." The old man sighed. "Now you want to go into the army. Let me think on it."

The next day William Parker spoke to his son. "Go, my boy. You have my permission to offer your services to your country. Follow your friend Grant. He will be a great leader. Follow him and you too will be a great war captain."

Chapter 13

CAPTAIN PARKER

THE CHIEF SACHEM of the Senecas was well known in Albany, and Ely had no trouble in being admitted to the Governor's office. He wasted no time in making his request.

"I would like a commission and authority to raise a regiment to fight for the Union. I feel I am well qualified as I am an engineer with considerable experience," he said.

The Governor looked up, but avoided his eyes. "I am sorry, but I have no place for you."

"No place for an engineer in an army that is crying for them?"

"There is no place for you," the Governor repeated.

Ely was surprised. He was no stranger to prejudice, but he had not expected such a reply. He renewed his request vigorously, pointing out again the desperate need for the skills of trained engineers. A few more minutes of discussion made him realize that the Governor would not change his mind. Ely left the city filled with rage. He wondered what the trouble was. Surely not simple prejudice, not the fact that he was Indian. White men had always been happy to have red men fight with them in their wars.

Soon he was in Washington. He stood before the Secretary of State, William H. Seward, and repeated his request. Seward's reply was prompt and direct. "This struggle is an affair between white men. The Indian is not called upon to act. The fight must be settled by white men."

"But I am an American. I am an engineer. I can help. Engineers are needed," Ely protested.

"We will settle our troubles without Indian aid."

"You already have Indian aid. So does the Confederacy. Indians are fighting on both sides."

"No. You are not needed."

"But I have resigned my position," Ely declared.

Do-ne-ho-ga-wa went back home. His rage disappeared as he recovered his self-control. He knew people were talking, saying he was a failure.

Three hundred Senecas volunteered as privates. Dr. Wilson, an Indian, had become an army surgeon. Yet Ely was not accepted. He didn't know why. Had he made enemies in his long fight for the Senecas? He had argued forcefully for them. He had hurt the financial interests and wounded the pride of

many of his opponents. Perhaps it was prejudice, distaste at the thought of a red man being in such an important post as an officer engineer.

His Indian friends, at least, should know what he had done for them. Yet some of them were talking about him. "He can't be much of a man to be refused by the army."

But he seemed not to know what they were saying. He was not yet through. He had not given up when he went back to school. Many people had thought he couldn't or wouldn't finish. He did not give up when he worked with Lewis Morgan trying to collect the story of a civilization. He did not give up in his long fight for the Tonawanda Senecas. He refused to stop his progress when he was denied admission to the bar. It is not easy to paddle a canoe upstream, but he would not give up now.

He sent letters to his friends, to Ulysses S. Grant. Days turned into weeks and months. Grant wanted engineers, but even a General was unable to overcome army red tape and the other pressures, whatever they were, that blocked his way.

Ely tended his farm and cared for his horses. Over two years after the war started, in June, 1863, an army officer rode into the field where the Chief Sachem of the Iroquois was cultivating corn.

The officer dismounted and saluted. "Mister Parker?" he asked.

Ely nodded. The officer handed him an envelope. It contained a commission. He had been appointed Captain. The doors of a new career opened.

Now, many of the Indians who had found fault with him who had said he must not be much of a man, changed their minds. Once again they praised him and pleaded with him not to leave them.

"This is not a boys' quarrel. It is a struggle of giants and our country is being ruined. I must do what I can," Ely said.

The Iroquois gathered and, repeating the ancient ceremonies, with songs and dancing and feasting, sent Do-ne-ho-ga-wa off to war.

Chapter 14

GENERAL GRANT'S MILITARY SECRETARY

CAPTAIN PARKER was ordered to report to General J. E. Smith. He worked in designing and preparing fortifications until September when new orders came to report to General Grant at Vicksburg. Already he had become known to General Smith as a "good engineer."

He rode up to General Grant's headquarters and dismounted.

"Ah, Wolf. Welcome," said General Grant. "It has taken me a long time to get you here."

"General," said Ely, "I am glad to join you. It will be my privilege to serve you."

"There is plenty for you to do—laying out defenses, helping with supplies. And above all, get rid of this army red tape. That is what has kept you away from me for so long. If good

engineering and a clear mind can do the job, you are the man for us here. Your penmanship is excellent too. Better than anyone we have on the staff. It will be a pleasure to sign orders that are well written." He put his arm on his friend's shoulder.

There was full understanding between Grant and Parker, and "The Indian," as Parker became known, was of great help to his commander.

Captain Parker laid out defenses by riding his big, black horse along the line to be fortified. With Indian wisdom of woods and streams and hills, he did better that way than others did with a transit and compass.

"You should be careful, Wolf. Your disregard of danger may result in injury," the General warned him.

"I do not believe that I am to be killed by a bullet. I propose to come through without a wound, even though my coat and hat may sometimes get a few bullet holes in them."

"You often ride in full view of the enemy and within his range," said Grant.

"I only follow your example."

"But it is my job."

"Mine too. How can we have fortifications or bridges or roads or whatever is needed if I do not show where they should be and supervise their building?" Ely replied.

He continued to go, without fear, wherever his duties took him. The black horse he rode was from his farm on the banks of the Tonawanda River, a good animal, large enough to carry with ease his tall, straight rider. That their size and style presented an inviting target never seemed to occur to the busy Captain.

If bullets didn't reach him, the fever did, twice. He disliked the medicine given, whiskey and quinine. He never forgot that alcohol was the drug that caused so much Indian distress.

"Give me the quinine. The whiskey I will not take," he told the doctor.

"You are a very sick Indian. If you don't take it, you may die," the doctor insisted.

"Of course I will die. The question is, when? We all have to die sooner or later, but I do not have to drink whiskey. I have never seen it do any good and I have seen it do a great deal of harm. I'll see what happens with the quinine and without the whiskey."

A year after he joined Grant's staff, Captain Parker was made a Lieutenant Colonel and the General's private military secretary. Now the relationship of the two men became even closer. Parker wrote messages and prepared orders for the General to sign. He attended to his personal mail. He seemed to know everything that was needed. His fine, clear handwriting was important in the prompt and efficient flow of work.

One day as he was working at Grant's writing table, a citizen at headquarters said he had seen the General when he first took command three years before. "I would like to see him again," he said.

"His quarters are right over there," a busy young officer said, pointing to the tent where Ely was working.

The man approached as close as he thought proper and peered under the open flaps of the tent. As he turned away, the young officer asked, "Did you see General Grant?"

"Yup. I saw him all right, but he sure is sunburned now," the man said.

President Lincoln visited General Grant's headquarters at City Point, Virginia, in the last week of March and the first week of April, 1865. Between conferences and inspections he sometimes shared the mess with the General and his staff.

Parker, whose mind was seldom far away from Indian problems, discussed his ideas of better treatment of the red men and improved handling of Indian affairs. Seeds were planted that would bear fruit a few years later.

Chapter 15

A CLOSE CALL

DURING THE Campaign of the Wilderness, Grant's army faced Richmond, Virginia. The countryside had been under heavy fire. The enemy's guns were close, behind thick patches of underbrush.

General Grant went on an inspection trip with five officers of his staff. The crack of rifle fire could be heard in the near distance. The going was hard. There was no trail. The party followed the General as he turned his horse this way and that way, to go around old trenches, blasted tree stumps, and fallen timbers.

Lieutenant Colonel Parker touched his spurs to his black horse's side and caught up with he General. "Do you know where you are, sir?" he asked. He didn't use his friend's first name in the company of others.

Grant pulled up his horse. He looked around. "I guess I could use some help. I'm afraid I don't know exactly where I

L.F.B.

am. In fact, I guess I'm lost," he said sheepishly after a long pause.

"Lost?" The others looked about nervously.

"Does anyone know how to get out of here?" someone asked. The woods suddenly seemed deathly still. It was as though the enemy was watching, waiting, ready to shoot.

"Wolf, you are an Indian. You must know something about woodcraft. What shall we do?"

"I haven't been in the woods very much since I was a boy," Ely answered, "but I learned never to go into strange country without watching carefully. I have been wondering when you were going to turn back north."

"North? Aren't we going north?"

"No indeed. And we must be almost within the enemy lines."

"Do you know which way to go?" the General asked anxiously.

"Yes, I do, General."

"Please take over then."

"Follow me, gentlemen," said the Chief Sachem of the Senecas. He turned the black horse, loosened the reins, and broke into a gallop over the rough land, the others following. In a few minutes the party was back within its own lines.

When the war was over, Ely met a Confederate officer who remembered the day. "We had you right in our sights," he told Parker.

Ely had known the party was near the enemy lines, but had not realized quite how close. He listened to the Confederate officer with interest.

"Yes," the man continued. "My men wanted to shoot, but I told them to wait. If you had kept on coming we would have captured all of you. I saw you catch up to the General and talk with him, then gallop off in haste with the rest following you. You were within forty rods and we hoped to get you all within the next five minutes."

Chapter 16

A SENECA AT APPOMATTOX

When the spring rains came in March, 1865, the Northern armies were drawing a circle around Confederate General Robert E. Lee's forces. Orders and letters poured out of Grant's headquarters. Many were written and signed by Lieutenant Colonel Ely S. Parker.

On April 9, the violence of war came to an end in the McLean farmhouse in the village of Appomattox Court House, Virginia, where Lee surrendered.

Colonel Charles Marshall was with Lee. General Grant arrived with Colonels Joe Bowers and Orville Babcock and Lieutenant Colonel Parker. Generals Sheridan, Ord, Porter, and other officers followed.

As General Grant wrote a short letter containing the terms of surrender, Parker was at his elbow, assisting in making corrections. Lee read the letter and wrote a letter of acceptance.

The bloody War Between the States was at the point of

ending. The leaders of the opposing armies were present, waiting. Grant asked Colonel Bowers, the Senior Adjutant, to write the documents in ink. Bowers took up the pen. His hand shook. He was so overwhelmed by the tense scene that he could not write.

Colonel Bowers, with trembling hands, gave the paper to Lieutenant Colonel Parker, who calmly sat at a small oval table and put down the words that marked the end of four years of bitter fighting.

Emotion did not pass him by. His feeling ran as high as the others. But he was Do-ne-ho-ga-wa, the Chief Sachem of the Senecas. The blood of the leaders of generations of Iroquois ran in his veins and gave him self-control and the appearance of calm.

His good penmanship had not left him. His eyes scanned the crisp, clean writing. The task done, he handed the paper to General Grant, who signed it. General Lee also signed the letter of acceptance. The war was over.

The Indian who had been told to go back to his farm while white men fought a white man's war had written out the terms of surrender.

General Grant introduced his officers to General Lee. When Lieutenant Colonel Parker was presented, Lee stared at him for a moment. Did he wonder at an Indian being present at such an important moment? Did he think of the others of color, of the blacks whose slavery he had defended, whose ancestors had come to America with the first white men?

He extended his hand and said, "I am glad to see one real American here."

Lieutenant Colonel Parker took the hand in his own. "We are all Americans," he said.

Chapter 17

COMMISSIONER OF INDIAN AFFAIRS

THE DAY of surrender and the days that followed saw more orders and letters from General Grant's headquarters that were signed by E. S. Parker. Ely was busy attending to the details of the disposition of two armies. Their movement to their homes was made possible. Food and supplies were delivered to the conquered. Prisoners were freed.

Colonel Parker remained with Grant after the war. He was made Brigadier General "for gallant and meritorious services."

A new law gave rights of citizenship to Indians who had fought in the war. Ely must have smiled ruefully at the irony of it when, as a reward for his services in the war, he was declared competent, although he was an Indian, to become a citizen and a voter.

Parker remained close to Grant in the years that followed.

But he was still Do-ne-ho-ga-wa, the Keeper of the Western Door of the Iroquois. He did not forget his Seneca people. He drafted legislation for the protection and improvement of the Tonawanda Senecas for the New York State legislature. He drew up the national laws of the Tribal Council.

In financial affairs Ely Parker was successful. Wise investments earned him a comfortable fortune. He married Miss Minnie Sackett on December 25, 1867. General Grant attended the wedding.

The government often sought General Parker's advice in Indian affairs, and assigned him to meet with Indian delegations to Washington. And often too, he went to Indian tribes as a government agent to treat with them at Grand Councils.

Ulysses S. Grant became President on March 4, 1869, and on April 13, he appointed Ely Parker as Commissioner of Indian Affairs, the first Indian to become Commissioner. Parker resigned as Brigadier General and began the work that was uppermost in his mind—the improvement of the lot of Indians. His ideas had already appeared in Grant's inaugural address and again in the President's first annual message to Congress.

The ideas Ely had developed sprang into action. First, the new Commissioner wanted the Indian to see himself as a useful member of society, to take his place in it and contribute to human welfare, and to help himself. He knew how difficult that would be, but he knew that it could be done. He himself had already done it.

Second, he wanted to impress on government departments the fact that the people of the United States owed the Indians a wholesome and clean administration of Indian affairs; that they should undertake to lift the red man out of the poverty into which he had been forced.

Close to the President, he could speak with him. "I want to develop an Indian Peace Policy," Parker said. "I want to uplift, at all cost, the native people of this land who have been robbed and whose lives have been ruined."

"Do so," said the President. "I have had experience in Indian country and in Indian wars. A completely new policy is necessary. The country has a moral duty to the Indians."

"And I think this might very well be done by use of outstanding, public-minded citizens, a Board of Indian Commissioners."

"A good idea. You will have my assistance."

"The system is corrupt. Goods for Indians in warehouses are stolen, and replaced with inferior material. Beef on the hoof is often delivered to Indian reservations and paid for by the government and distributed to the Indians. Then the cattle are stolen and delivered to another reservation. If they are not stolen they are sometimes bought back from the Indians, first made drunk, for a cheap trinket and a bottle of whiskey. Fraud is at every hand."

"I know," said the President. "I have often met with fraud in the purchase of army supplies. You will need to be alert."

"Men who do such things have money. There is bribery. I have seen the tricks all of my life. There is a great need for an alert, honest board of citizens to watch the scoundrels and keep close check on business proceedures, on purchases, deliveries, quality. The board may be asked to help select new Indian agents."

"Your ideas are good. I approve of them. I will support them," said the President.

President Grant appointed the board. The new Commissioner carefully instructed its members. New Indian agents were appointed.

A stiff new broom was at work. The new Indian Peace Policy was in effect.

Chapter 18

CHALLENGE BY RED CLOUD

Do-ne-ho-ga-wa's heart was glad. As Commissioner of Indian Affairs, he was in a position to do a great deal of good for America's red men.

The news soon spread through the Indian country. The tribes were told there was a new Great White Father in Washington. They were told he had selected a red man to be their Little White Father. It was hard to believe. After so many years of deceit by white men, could it be possible their affairs were to be handled by an Indian?

White men seemed to be born with a feather between their fingers and a paper in their hands. The Great Spirit had at last remembered his red children and had put a red man in a place of power.

The first year after Parker was appointed there were no large-scale Indian wars, although the angry crack of rifle fire was sometimes heard as small military and Indian forces came against each other during the uneasy peace.

Some army officers did not approve of the Peace Policy. Their views were shared by some businessmen and politicians. In spite of the official policy, strong influences were still opposed to any change.

The army was in control of the vast western lands. Military force was used to police Indian country. It was pushing against the Sioux, the Northern Cheyennes, and other tribes, trying to get them to go to a reservation on the Missouri River near Fort Randall.

The Indians resisted. Fort Randall was three hundred miles from their homes and was in an area where game was scarce. The Indians were told that treaties they had signed in 1866 and 1868 required them to move.

"Lies!" Red Cloud, the Oglala Sioux chief, cried.

The building of the Union Pacific Railroad and the slaughter of the giant herds of buffalo had made the Indians alert to the ambitions of the whites.

Gold was discovered in Montana in 1862. By 1864, the Bozeman Trail from western Nebraska was established. It ran through the heart of the Indian country, across the valleys of the Powder, the Tongue, and the Big Horn Rivers. The building of new forts to protect the trail was begun.

At the signing of the treaty in 1866, the Indians were told that the government did not want to buy their land, but only wanted peace and the right to use the Bozeman Trail; that travelers would not kill game. Not much was said about the other complicated provisions of the treaty, which permitted the removal of the Indians.

Spotted Tail, chief of the Brulé Sioux, and others signed the treaty in view of the promises made. Red Cloud had heard the white man's promises before. He had seen them broken, and he had not forgotten. He would not sign.

War flamed from the Platte to the Yellowstone. Pressures by the army, settlers, and government agents continued. Finally, in 1868, after more promises that the Bozeman road would not be developed without consent of the Indians, that they would not be forced to move from their Powder River hunting grounds, Red Cloud reluctantly put his mark to a treaty. So did Spotted Tail. The Indians thought they would be left alone, that they could trade at Fort Laramie and that they would be given ammunition for hunting.

But government agents still insisted on the move. Little wonder Red Cloud spoke as he did.

"Lies! All lies! You told me I would not have to move!" Hundreds of braves back of him grimly looked to their rifles and war paint and muttered about the white man's forked tongue. Their hearts were bad. A climax was building. War loomed.

Red Cloud refused to move. He wanted to stay where he was, on the Powder River. He wanted to do his trading at Fort Laramie, near his hunting grounds.

Do-ne-ho-ga-wa heard of Red Cloud's rising anger. Glowing sparks of bitterness would soon burst into flame unless something was done.

He asked Red Cloud and Spotted Tail to come to Washington. Spotted Tail and his group arrived first. A week later, on June 1, 1870, Red Cloud with a party of twenty-four chiefs, braves, and interpreters, and the wives of four of the Indians stepped off the train in Washington.

The new Commissioner met them as a friend. "I am very glad to see you today," he said when he met them. "I am glad you have had no accident and that you have arrived here all safe. I want to hear what Red Cloud has to say for himself and his people."

Red Cloud answered, "I do not want my reservation on the Missouri. I was born in the land above the forks of the Platte and I was told that land belonged to me. When you send goods to me they are stolen. They held a paper for me to sign and that is all I got for my land. I know the people you send out are liars. I do not want war. I want you to tell all of this to the Great White Father."

"I will do my best," said Do-ne-ho-ga-wa.

Red Cloud continued. "Grant my people the powder they need. All I ask is for enough for my people to kill game."

The Indians were taken to see the sights in Washington. They were entertained at the White House. They enjoyed the food, especially the strawberries and ice cream. "Surely

L.F.B.

the white men have many more good things to eat than they send to the Indians," Spotted Tail said as he looked at the loaded banquet table.

The western visitors all wanted to speak to their new Little White Father. Of all the marvels of Washington, that, they thought, was the greatest. An Indian Little White Father! Really, a Little Red Father.

President Grant and Secretary of Interior Jacob Cox spoke to them. When the Indians signed the treaties of 1866 and 1868, they agreed to move if the government asked. The officials pointed to the writing in the papers.

Not so, the Indians declared. They thought they were signing treaties of peace and trade. They didn't know the government might require them to move away from their homes. These white men, with a feather between their fingers!

Red Cloud declared, "I signed a treaty of peace. Not this treaty. No one told me about this. I cannot read and write your language. I will not move. It is all lies! We will leave now and go home!"

Do-ne-ho-ga-wa talked to President Grant and Secretary Cox. He explained that war would come if the Indians were forced to move. The interpreters of the treaties had lied to the red men. Few men knew better than he how such treaties were made. He had studied them and had fought against them most of his life.

He suggested a solution. The Powder River country, north

of the Platte, had herds of buffalo which the Indians needed for food. Let it be their hunting ground. They could live there or on the reservation, just as they wished. That would be fair.

After Red Cloud heard the new interpretation of the treaty, he said to the Commissioner, "Yesterday, when I saw the treaty and all the false things in it, I was mad, and I suppose it made you the same. Now I am pleased."

Do-ne-ho-ga-wa's sincerity and fairness had prevented war.

Chapter 19

FALSE CHARGES

OTHER CHIEFS listened to the voice of the new Great White Father. They knew that the Little White Father had a single tongue. No forked tongue there. What he did, what he said, went into the deepest, darkest corners of Indian affairs, like a breath of fresh, spring air.

Commissioner Parker realized the ancient days of the Indian were going fast. Soon they would be gone and would never return. The problem was to treat the red men fairly and honestly, to make it possible for them to live decently in the new world that was overtaking them, to join it, to become citizens, not victims.

It was not an easy road. Grafting contractors began to find that they were losing fraudulent profits. They developed new schemes to cheat both the Indians and the government.

If the doors to dishonest profits were closed to them, there was another way. Attack the Commissioner. That is what hap-

pened. Ely Parker himself was accused of fraud.

He had been in office little more than a year. Accusations by his enemies filled the air. He was called "one who is but a remove from barbarism." He was called "a bad Indian."

And there was the demand: "The Indian must be put out."

Parker's answer was to open his books at once, his personal records as well as those of the Indian Office. The investigators thumbed through them. There was the small but comfortable fortune his salary and carefully selected investments had earned him.

All of the thirteen charges made against him fell, one by one. He was tried before a Committee of the House of Representatives in February, 1871. The clear purpose behind the charges was to ruin the Indian.

The Committee made its report: "Your committee have not found evidence of fraud or corruption on the part of the Indian Commissioner. . . . We have found no evidence of any pecuniary advantage sought or derived by the Commissioner or any one connected with the bureau."

Commissioner Parker had held his office for almost two years. During that time there were no major Indian wars. The smoke of peace rose from the campfires.

Chapter 20

THE COMMISSIONER RESIGNS

THE APPEARANCE of calm did not leave Ely, but he was filled with rage and dismay.

"I don't see how I can stay," he told the President.

"It will be difficult, but why not?" the President asked.

"Corruption does not die easily. More attacks will come."

"You can defend yourself again."

"Perhaps, but at the cost of time and money. They will frame me. Besides that, how can my promises be kept?"

"I will keep them."

"But you will not be President forever. And when you were a General, you could not conquer either red tape or fraud. That was when we were at war. Now we are dealing with corruption. It is still war. But the enemy is more difficult to defeat. He may even be disguised as a friend," Ely said.

"We must keep on trying."

"That is true. But it goes deeper. Red Cloud, for example.

We are at peace with him. He trusted me. How can I prevent some army unit from a massacre of Indians? Not even you can prevent it. There will be false reports and false witnesses."

The President said, "Perhaps we can win this. The Peace Policy has great public approval."

"It has the approval of the gentle, the kind, the thoughtful people of good will. Many of our citizens do not know of it, others do not understand it. And some men who are powerful in politics and business and the professions are against it. The forces of corruption are strong and they will not relent."

"We cannot stop."

"Exactly. But I am an Indian. Your enemies will fight me relentlessly. It will cause you only embarrassment if I remain in office. I think you can do better without me. The color of my skin angers them. When corrupt men attack me, when they frame me—as they most certainly will—they will be attacking you. I don't want that. You will have enough problems without bearing those created because I am an Indian. I don't want to cause you more trouble than you would have without me in office. No. I must resign."

It was a heartbreaking conclusion. Ely had felt so much pleasure with his chance to help his people and his nation, but now he saw it was hopeless.

"If you say so, Wolf. But I will miss you. Our friendship, born in our youth, has grown through the years of war and politics. Yes, indeed. I will miss you."

In New York, after his resignation, Ely Parker practiced his profession of engineering and did well. His fortune increased. He built a country home in Fairfield, Connecticut. He moved in good society. His wife was ill much of the time, but he found great comfort in his family life, with his wife and his daughter, Maud.

Then another blow came. He had signed a bond for a friend, a banker. The friend needed money and stole from his bank. General Parker was called to make good on his bond.

"You don't have to pay," his attorney said. "You are an Indian."

"Yes. I am an Indian, and therefore I must pay. I could not live with myself if I did not," Parker replied.

"But the law protects you. A contract with an Indian cannot be enforced. No one can make you pay."

"I signed the bond, and I will pay. If the law does not compel me, my honor does."

It was a financial blow he never recovered from. The crash of the Freedman's Bank, followed by the failure of an insurance company and a publishing business in which he had invested, made him a poor man.

He took a position as architect in the New York City Police Department. His fortune had slipped away from him, but his engineering training and his wide experience left him with his self-respect and the means of earning a living as old age came upon him.

Chapter 21

DO-NE-HO-GA-WA GOES HOME

Do-ne-ho-ga-wa, always faithful to the Iroquois and their memory, joined other Indians and white people in establishing a memorial to Red Jacket, the famous Seneca orator. It was erected in Forest Lawn Cemetary in Buffalo on land where the ancient Senecas had lived.

The Keeper of the Western Door of the Iroquois found, in the words of Red Jacket, the history of the Iroquois:

"I am an aged tree, and can stand no longer. My leaves are fallen. My branches are withered and I am shaken by every breeze. Soon my aged trunk will be prostrate."

The Iroquois Confederacy was also old, its warriors were going, the tribes were fading away. Soon the ancient Indian society would be no more.

Time was running out for Ely Parker too. Another strong branch was shaken. It fell on August 31, 1895, when Do-ne-ho-ga-wa died.

The Red Jacket silver medal from General Washington, and the sacred wampum, symbols of his title and authority, were displayed at his funeral service. He was buried in Fairfield, Connecticut. In the old days that land had been Pequot territory and they had been vassals of the Iroquois. It was not a fitting place for the grave of Do-ne-ho-ga-wa, the Chief Sachem of the Iroquois and the Guardian of the Western Door. And the prophecy of his mother's dream was unfulfilled.

The Great Spirit, with the floating spirits of the unseen, moved ten years later. His mother's dream would come true—all of it. The ancient land of his ancestors would indeed fold him in death as the dream reader had said.

The Buffalo Historical Society, with the consent of Mrs. Parker, moved the body of Do-ne-ho-ga-wa from the land of the Pequots to the Red Jacket Memorial in Buffalo. There it was placed in the sacred soil of the Senecas at the spot seen by his mother in her dream.

Ely Parker's life was guided by the Iroquois rule: "Spend no time in mourning the failures of the past. Tears make a bitter throat. Look ahead, there is more work to do. Unstop your ears and listen. Hear the call."

INDEX

THE AUTHOR

Harold W. Felton, a lawyer by profession, is an author known for his tall tales and his biographies for young readers. A long-time interest in American folklore led to the first of his widely acclaimed books, an anthology of legends about Paul Bunyan. Since that time he has pursued folk heroes with enthusiasm, and his stories about Pecos Bill, John Henry, Gib Morgan, and others rank him as a master yarn-spinner.

In his book about the horse named Justin Morgan, Mr. Felton dealt with facts that seemed like tall tales—history that was "almost too good to be true." Turning to the lives of Jim Beckwourth, Nat Love, Elizabeth Freeman, and James Weldon Johnson, he discovered the same sort of material—biographies more astonishing than fiction.

Long a resident of New York City, Mr. Felton and his wife now reside in Falls Village, Connecticut.

THE ILLUSTRATOR

Lorence F. Bjorklund has illustrated numerous books, both adult and juvenile titles, and many of them have had to do with American Indians and the West which he knows so well. He has written and illustrated his own book, Faces of the Frontier, and collaborated with his daughter in preparing The Indians of Northeastern America.

Born in Minnesota, Mr. Bjorklund grew up in St. Paul. A scholarship to Pratt Institute brought him to New York, where he earned a living drawing illustrations for the then popular Western magazines. Today, he and his wife live in Croton Falls, New York, with summers spent in South Thomaston, Maine.